THE TAO OF MA'AT

Nekhen M. Asar
Kevin L. Michel

Copyright © 2025 Kevin L. Michel

All rights reserved

No part of this book may be reproduced, or stored in a retrieval system, or transmitted in any form or by any means, electronic, mechanical, photocopying, recording, or otherwise, without express written permission of the publisher.

CONTENTS

Title Page
Copyright
The Balance   1
I.
The Path   2
II.
Silence   3
III.
Humility   4
IV.
Truth   5
V.
Speech   6
VI.
Quenching the Coal   7
VII.
Patience   8
VIII.

Justice	9
IX. Pride	10
X. The Jar by the Door	11
XI. Friendship	12
XII. The Ancestors	13
XIII. Diligence	14
XIV. Joy	15
XV. Moderation	16
XVI. Mercy	17
XVII. Judgment	18
XVIII. The Shepherd's Staff	19
XIX. Grain and Gold	20
XX. Family	21
XXI. Marriage	22

XXII. Envy	23
XXIII. Forethought	24
XXIV. Desire	25
XXV. Wisdom	26
XXVI. Mortality	27
XXVII. Legacy	28
XXVIII. Two Voices	29
XXIX. The Cry for Justice	30
XXX. Nature	31
XXXI. Change	32
XXXII. Homecoming	33
XXXIII. Purpose	34
XXXIV. Integrity	35
XXXV.	

XXXVI. Community	36
XXXVII. Old Age	37
XXXVIII. Health	38
XXXIX. Confession	39
XL. Mind	40
XLI. Simplicity	41
XLII. Divine Justice	42
XLIII. Meddling	43
XLIV. Courage	44
XLV. Responding to Evil	45
XLVI. Perseverance	46
XLVII. Quarrel	47
XLVIII. Reverence	48
Teaching	49

XLIX. Honor	50
L. The Crowd	51
LI. Action	52
LII. Bad Company	53
LIII. Trust	54
LIV. Dignity	55
LV. Openness	56
LVI. Grief	57
LVII. Flattery	58
LVIII. Perspective	59
LIX. Everyday Ma'at	60
LX. Responsibility	61
LXI. Compassion	62
LXII.	

Laughter	63
LXIII. Gratitude	64
LXIV. Solitude	65
LXV. Oneness	66
LXVI. Self-Knowledge	67
LXVII. Excellence	68
LXVIII. Renewal	69
LXIX. Acceptance	70
LXX. Reflection	71
LXXI. Virtue	72
LXXII. Order	73
LXXIII. Example	74
LXXIV. Appearances	75
LXXV. Industry	76

LXXVI. Counsel	77
LXXVII. Understanding	78
LXXVIII. The Scales	79
LXXIX. Ma'at	80
LXXX. The Sage	81
LXXXI.	

THE BALANCE
I.

In the silence before dawn, the world hangs in perfect balance.

Ma'at, the unseen order, renews itself each day – great and unshaken since the first sunrise.

As the feather keeps the scale true, so does truth sustain sky and earth.

Walk gently in this balance – neither at war with the world, nor idle within it –

and you will find the path of Ma'at beneath your feet.

THE PATH
II.

Do not chase Ma'at with anxious hands; it is not a trophy to seize.
Ma'at is a path unwinding under humble feet, a current carrying the unresisting heart.
The harder you grasp the world, the more it slips away; the more gently you hold it, the more it supports you.
Be as the river reed – yielding, yet rooted in truth – and you will outlast the flood.

SILENCE
III.

Words have fire; silence has light.
In a council of noise, the quiet one hears clearly.
The fool's voice is loud, declaring his own wisdom;
the sage's voice is soft, asking to learn.
Be swift to listen, slow to proclaim.
Like a deep well, the still heart reflects the sky,
while the agitated heart churns up only mud.

HUMILITY
IV.

Do not let knowledge swell the heart.
No person knows every secret; we are all students under the sky.
Listen for wisdom in every voice – a peasant's truth can surpass a prince's folly.
The river of knowledge has many sources: clear water may spring from a humble well.
Bend your ear low to the ground of life; the seeds of insight often sprout in unlikely soil.

TRUTH
V.

Falsehood comforts for a moment, then crumbles.
Truth is a foundation stone from first dawn.
To live in truth is to live in light.
Even if the light is gentle at times, it never wavers.
A heart guided by truth fears no judgment; in the end,
Ma'at's feather finds it pure.

SPEECH VI.

Words can warm, words can burn.
A kind word can nourish a heart for years; a cruel word can scar it for a lifetime.
Before you let words fly, weigh them on the scale of your heart – will they build, or will they burn?
Speak plainly and with care.
Let your tongue be a tool to heal, not a dagger to wound.
In the mouth of the wise, words are a salve; in the mouth of the reckless, a poison.

QUENCHING THE COAL
VII.

When fire rises, do not feed it.
Close the mouth, slow the breath.
Let the flame eat its own smoke.
A moment of restraint
saves a year of repair.

PATIENCE
VIII.

As the sun takes time to climb the sky, so good things come in their season.

Rushing a task spoils its fruit; impatience is a drought that cracks the soul's soil.

Wait for the right moment, as the farmer waits for the flood to recede before sowing.

To be patient is not to do nothing, but to do what is right at the right pace.

Ma'at rewards the heart that can wait without wavering.

JUSTICE IX.

Do not tilt the scales against the helpless.
The orphan, the widow, the stranger – Ma'at hears their silent plea.
If you take from the poor to fatten yourself, you feed on poison.
Wealth gained by injustice is a pyramid built on sand: it will collapse and bury you.
True justice shines like the sun on all, without favor.
The breath of the divine lives in the cry of the wronged – take care lest it blow against you.

PRIDE
X.

Take care at your moment of triumph.
When the lotus blooms brightest, it forgets the mud that nurtured it.
Pride bloats the heart and blinds the mind.
A king on his throne still stands upon the earth – a single crack in the ground can bring him down.
Remember your beginnings when you reach the summit. Bow your head even at your highest, for the gods favor the modest.
The mountain does not mock the valley; it knows that, with time, even stone wears away.

THE JAR BY THE DOOR
XI.

At the door of a humble house sits a jar of cool water.

Each morning the householder fills it, though no traveler may come.

He asks nothing in return; his heart is light knowing a wanderer's thirst might be eased.

Charity is a quiet ripple in the pond of eternity.

The giver, the receiver, and the water itself are blessed in the act.

In giving, he serves Ma'at; in caring, he becomes part of the divine balance.

FRIENDSHIP
XII.

Friendship is a garden that must be tended.

Choose friends not for fine garments or rank, but for the goodness of their heart.

One faithful friend shelters you from a hundred storms; one false friend can betray you to ruin.

Be loyal and gentle with those you hold dear. Speak truth to them and defend them when they are absent.

In prosperity and adversity, a true friend walks beside you. Their footsteps match yours on the path of Ma'at.

THE ANCESTORS XIII.

In the ruins of old tombs, wisdom is carved on stone.
Heed the counsel of those who came before.
They built the first roads; their failures and triumphs paved your way.
By studying yesterday, you may foresee tomorrow.
Emulate the best in your forebears and learn from their mistakes.
Thus you honor their spirits and continue their story.
The one who remembers their roots stands firm against the fiercest wind.

DILIGENCE
XIV.

Perform your labor with a willing heart.

The farmer who rises before dawn reaps a bountiful harvest, while the sluggard curses an empty field.

Do your duty even when no eyes watch – Ma'at sees in secret and rewards the sincere.

To work with skill is to honor the gifts you have been given.

Do not disdain small tasks; a single brick laid each day builds a temple over years.

Diligence in humble work is better than shirking a great duty.

JOY
XV.

Do not spend all your days in gloom, nor all in mirth.

All toil and no laughter makes a life a burden; all play and no purpose leaves a life empty.

Find joy in small blessings – a cool breeze at noon, a shared smile.

Better a simple meal with a glad heart than a feast eaten in bitterness.

Gratitude turns what you have into enough.

When your heart is at peace with its portion, the gods themselves smile with you.

MODERATION XVI.

The cup that is overfilled spills on the ground.
Take your portion and be satisfied.
If you dine at a rich table, restrain your appetite; do not grasp at morsels with greedy hands.
Excess is the enemy of well-being: the body bloated with indulgence houses a restless spirit.
Eat until you are nourished, drink until your thirst is eased, and let contentment halt your hand.
A small measure enjoyed in peace outlasts a banquet devoured in haste.

MERCY XVII.

When wronged, the heart burns for revenge – but vengeance only doubles the bitterness.

To forgive is to pour cool water over flames.

It is the wise who mend a broken friendship while the foolish cling to pride.

Justice does not forbid mercy: punish when you must, but do not let hatred poison you.

By showing mercy to others, you heal your own soul.

The one who forgives carries a lighter heart and walks closer to Ma'at.

JUDGMENT XVIII.

When sitting in judgment, be as an impartial scale.
Listen to all sides before you decide; an answer given before hearing is a misshapen verdict.
Anger and favoritism are weights that tip the balance – remove them.
Let your mind be still and your heart steady.
Judge as you would wish to be judged.
Remember: all stand equal in the Hall of Truth when hearts are weighed.
If you stray from justice now, your own heart will bear the weight later.

THE SHEPHERD'S STAFF
XIX.

If you hold power, hold it lightly.
A ruler is keeper, not owner.
Guide with a staff, not a whip.
Be fair, be seen, be brief.
When you depart, let justice remain.

GRAIN AND GOLD
XX.

Do not boast in full granaries,
do not despair in lean years.
Better a crust in peace
than a chest that howls.
Open your store,
and sleep unguarded.

FAMILY
XXI.

Honor those who gave you life.
Respect your father's wisdom and your mother's love – these were your first guides.
Nurture your children with gentleness and good counsel; they carry your name into the future.
Quarrel not with siblings over trifles; a family united can weather any storm.
A home built on love and respect is a fortress no wind can overturn.
In the evening of life, the memory of harmony at home is a treasure beyond gold.

MARRIAGE XXII.

When you take a partner in life, let love and fidelity guide you.

Treat your spouse with reverence and kindness, as your own heart.

Do not dominate, nor neglect – a household thrives on mutual care.

Provide for your companion's needs and delight in their happiness.

A marriage founded on trust is a boat that can sail any river.

When there is disagreement, speak without scorn and listen without defense.

Two hearts in harmony create an enduring home.

ENVY
XXIII.

Chasing another man's star will only lead you astray.
Envy is a shadow that clouds the eye, making sweet things taste bitter.
Rejoice in your own blessings and they will grow.
The fruit on your neighbor's tree may look golden, but every garden has its hidden thorns.
By coveting what is not yours, you invite sorrow into your heart.
Keep your gaze on your own path – Ma'at has given you what you need for your journey.

FORETHOUGHT XXIV.

The wise plan for tomorrow even as they live fully today.

Before you build, envision the house; before you speak, imagine the echo.

A moment of thought can prevent an hour of regret.

Foresight is a lamp in the darkness of uncertainty.

Do not fear to dream and design, but also prepare for the unexpected storm.

Let your plans be as flexible as the river's course – bending around obstacles, yet ever flowing toward its goal.

By planting seeds of forethought, you harvest fields of peace.

DESIRE XXV.

Desire stirs like a great wind in the soul.
If left unchecked, it can capsize the boat of reason.
Acknowledge your desires, but steer them with a firm hand.
Do not let fleeting pleasures lure you off the path of Ma'at.
The sweet smell of the lotus can hide a pit of quicksand beneath.
Enjoy life's gifts in measure, without becoming their slave.
Self-control is the staff that supports you on the long journey – with it in hand, you walk free of entanglement.

WISDOM XXVI.

A fool thinks he is perfect; a wise person knows they are not.

The fool takes pride in loud opinions; the wise asks questions in quiet.

Wisdom is more listening than speaking.

It grows not from age alone, but from an open heart and mind.

The river of knowledge flows into the sea of wisdom only when the channels of pride are cleared.

Do not be wise in your own eyes.

Seek counsel and ponder deeply – wisdom will enter your soul like the dawn.

MORTALITY XXVII.

All who walk under the sun will one day walk into the west.
Death is as natural as sunset after day.
Do not fear it, but live so that when it comes, your heart is light.
No riches accompany you beyond the tomb; only the tale of your deeds echoes in eternity.
Let that tale be one of kindness and courage.
One who is mindful of death lives more fully – each day becomes a precious gift, not a right.

LEGACY
XXVIII.

No one lives forever, but a name can outlive the flesh.

What will your name mean when it is spoken after you are gone?

Monuments of stone crumble, but deeds of goodness remain in stories and hearts.

Kindness to a stranger, wisdom shared with a child, justice done in secret – these are bricks in the house of your legacy.

Writings may fade and statues fall, but the memory of virtue endures in the soul of the living.

Live so that long after your departure, the echo of your life gives others courage.

TWO VOICES
XXIX.

I said to my soul in sorrow:
"Better to end this life than to endure such pain.
My heart is weary; my name feels lost,
my lot is endless suffering with no friend to hear my cry –
like a bird trapped in a sunless twilight."
And my soul answered:
"Pain is a night that passes.
Death will come in its time; do not hasten it.
A day of clarity will follow this day of clouds.
Live now, do good now, and trust the dawn to come.
When your hour arrives, we will go together –
your heart at peace, your deeds shining behind you."

THE CRY FOR JUSTICE
XXX.

In a hall of granite and gold, a peasant stood trembling yet unyielding.

He had been robbed by a wicked hand, and no one would hear him.

Day after day, he returned to the gates of the great house; his voice grew hoarse, yet stronger with truth.

The eloquence of the wronged pierced the steward's heart, and at last the scales were set right.

Do not underestimate the power of a single honest voice.

Ma'at walks with the one who stands up for the right, even when he stands alone.

NATURE XXXI.

The natural world is a scroll of divine teachings.
Consider the stars: though distant and silent, they move in harmony each night.
Consider the Nile: it rises and falls with patience, bringing life without asking praise.
Trees give shade and fruit, asking nothing in return.
Animals live by their design, not by malice or greed.
Learn from these examples written by the Creator's hand: live simply, give freely, take only what you need.
If you care for the earth and its creatures, you keep Ma'at in your heart.
All life breathes beneath the same sky – walk gently among your fellow beings.

CHANGE XXXII.

No state is eternal under the sun.
Day turns to night, winter to spring, each in its season.
Rejoice not overmuch in good fortune, nor despair too deeply in misfortune.
The wheel of life turns, raising some up and bringing others low.
If today you are strong, use your strength kindly, for tomorrow you may need kindness.
If today you mourn, keep hope in your heart, for joy will find you again.
Nothing is permanent except Ma'at itself – the order that brings change into meaning.
Trust that order, and let each moment come and go like the tides.

HOMECOMING XXXIII.

A man fled his homeland when fear overtook him.
In foreign lands he gained wealth and honor, yet each night his dreams were of the river and fields of his youth.
No glory abroad could fill the void in his heart.
At last he returned home, bowing before his rightful lord, and was received with mercy.
Only then did he find the peace that had eluded him.
The heart, like a bird, eventually flies back to where it belongs.
Truth and belonging awaited him where he began.

PURPOSE
XXXIV.

Each heart beats with a purpose set by the divine.
Do not ignore the calling that makes your spirit sing.
If your gift is to craft, then craft with devotion; if to heal, then heal with compassion.
A life without purpose is a ship without a rudder – adrift and aimless.
Time is the most precious gift; wasting it is an insult to the spirit.
Work at what brings you and others real good.
Thus when your days draw to a close, you will rest content,
knowing you lived true to the song in your heart.

INTEGRITY XXXV.

Be the same person in darkness as you are in light.
Let integrity be a straight rod that does not bend in the wind.
If offered a bribe, reject it as you would a cup of poison.
Ill-gotten gains turn to dust, while a clean conscience is a soft pillow.
Speak truth even when it costs you, and do right even when none see.
The true judge of your deeds is the heart within.
Keep your integrity, and your heart will rest easy under the stars.

COMMUNITY XXXVI.

No one is an island entire of itself.

As villagers join to raise a house, so we need one another.

Offer help freely to your neighbors, and accept help humbly in turn.

Do not isolate yourself in pride or fear.

Sharing burdens makes them lighter; sharing joys makes them brighter.

A community in harmony is like a boat crew rowing in time: their journey is swift and smooth.

Contribute your strength to the common good, and you strengthen yourself as well.

Weave yourself gently into the lives of others, and you will find Ma'at in the bonds between hearts.

OLD AGE
XXXVII.

Age creeps upon us like the slow rising of the Nile.
One day you find your hair a river of gray and your back bent like a bow.
Do not lament getting older – each year is a harvest of lessons.
In youth one has vigor; in age one gains perspective.
Respect the elderly, for they have traveled roads you have yet to walk.
As you age, do not cling to youth's glories; embrace the role of guide and storyteller.
A sunset has its own beauty no sunrise can rival.
In life's cycle, old age is not an end but the season of wisdom.

HEALTH XXXVIII.

Your body is the vessel carrying your spirit through this journey.
Treat it with respect and balance.
Eat wholesome foods, but do not live to eat.
Move your limbs so they remain strong, but let vanity not be your master.
Avoid excesses that dull the mind or weaken the heart.
Rest when you are weary – even the lion must sleep.
Do not poison yourself with what you know will harm you.
A clear mind dwells in a healthy body.
By caring for your body, you honor the gift of life that Ma'at has given.

CONFESSION XXXIX.

To admit a fault is the first step to healing.
Even the righteous heart errs at times.
Do not persist in a lie to save face – hidden rot only spreads unseen.
Stand before your own heart and speak the truth of your deeds.
Ask forgiveness where you have harmed, and make right what you can.
The gods know we are not perfect; they value the sincere, not the falsely perfect.
In the Hall of Truth, better to have stumbled and confessed
than to wear a mask of virtue over a corrupted heart.

MIND
XL.

As you think, so you become.
The mind is a garden that can grow flowers or weeds.
Nurture thoughts of compassion, fairness, and hope, and pluck out envy, fear, and despair as they sprout.
What you allow to take root in your mind will bear fruit in your life.
Do not dwell on anxious fantasies or bitter memories; let the present be your field of focus.
Keep your thoughts aligned with Ma'at and you will know inner harmony.
A balanced mind gives birth to a balanced life.

SIMPLICITY
XLI.

The sweetest water comes from a humble spring.
Live simply, that you may live freely.
Pride in fine garments and ornate palaces is a burden to the soul.
Better a small hut where you laugh than a grand house where you cry.
Possessions, once beyond need, begin to possess you.
Let your heart be light and your footprint gentle on the earth.
Owning little, you have nothing to fear losing.
The wealth of a simple life is contentment and peace – treasures no thief can steal and no time can rust.

DIVINE JUSTICE XLII.

Do not be troubled if evildoers prosper for a time.
Their shadows lengthen at evening; night will catch up to them.
The hidden hand of heaven balances the scales when mortals cannot.
An unjust man may sleep on silk, but his dreams are filled with jackals;
a just man may sleep on straw, but his heart rests easy.
Fret not at the delay of justice – the scales of heaven may shift slowly, but they settle true.
In the end, every deed meets its due.
Trust that Ma'at prevails beyond what your eyes can see.

MEDDLING
XLIII.

Do not poke your nose into every quarrel or secret.
One who grabs a stray dog by the ears invites a bite; so does one who leaps into others' disputes invite trouble.
Offer advice when asked, not before.
Keep confidence with what is told in trust – gossip is a knife that cuts both speaker and subject.
Mind your own tasks and let others manage theirs unless great harm would follow your silence.
By avoiding meddling, you keep your peace and earn trust.
The quiet bystander often sees more clearly than the noisy interferer.

COURAGE
XLIV.

Fear is a shadow that shrinks the heart.
Some fear is natural and keeps us safe; too much fear binds us like a prison.
To live rightly, one must sometimes walk through fear as through a dark tunnel, trusting light ahead.
Courage is not the absence of fear, but action in spite of it.
Call upon Ma'at when your knees tremble – remember the justice and truth you stand for.
Better to fail doing right than to succeed through cowardice.
A lion may sleep in your heart; rouse it when needed.
Each act of courage feeds the soul, and fear flees from a steadfast heart.

RESPONDING TO EVIL
XLV.

If another does evil to you, do not mirror his deeds.
To meet darkness with darkness only deepens the night.
Resist the urge to strike back in kind; instead, stand firm in the light of Ma'at.
Repay cruelty with fairness, and hatred with dignity.
This is not surrender to wrong, but rising above it.
By not becoming what you hate, you break the cycle.
One who stays righteous in the face of wickedness is shielded by the unseen.
In the contest between good and evil, one heart steadfast in good can tip the balance.

PERSEVERANCE XLVI.

When you embark on a worthy endeavor, persevere through difficulty.

The stone is shaped to a statue by many steady strokes, not one blow.

If you stumble, do not be ashamed – pick yourself up and continue.

Obstacles test your resolve: the easy path often leads nowhere.

Be patient as the eagle circling high, waiting for the right moment to strike.

Great achievements are collections of small actions done faithfully each day.

Do not let setbacks break your spirit. Rest if you must, but do not give up the journey.

Ma'at favors the soul that keeps walking forward, even on rough ground.

QUARREL XLVII.

Avoid a senseless quarrel as you would avoid a cobra.
Many angry words solve nothing and leave lasting wounds.
If you disagree, speak calmly and listen deeply.
Sometimes yielding a small point wins a greater peace.
Do not pour oil on the fire of another's rage; stay composed and gentle.
Consider: is your goal to prove yourself right, or to find the truth?
Pride makes us fight for an empty victory.
Step back and let tempers cool – a dispute often softens with time and understanding.
Wise are those who defer their wrath and seek common ground under Ma'at.

REVERENCE XLVIII.

Life is sacred; treat it as such.
When you approach the temple or the tomb, do so with a clean heart.
Speak no blasphemy; make no oath lightly.
The statues and symbols are stone and wood, but what they represent is eternal.
Offer sincere prayers, not just ritual words.
Honor the sacred in others – the divine spark in each heart.
Reverence is not fear, but profound respect for what is greater than yourself.
Walk gently under heaven's gaze, and let your life be an offering of truth.

TEACHING XLIX.

Knowledge is a candle – lighting another's wick does not dim your own flame.
Share what you know with those who seek wisdom.
A teacher once helped you take your first steps; honor them by guiding another.
Be patient with the student who struggles, for even the mighty oak begins as a tender shoot.
In teaching, you learn; in giving, you receive.
Hide not your wisdom out of jealousy or pride – that is hoarding grain while others starve.
Let your teachings be true and kind, a beacon not a burden.
Thus you keep the flame of Ma'at burning bright through the generations.

HONOR L.

In both victory and defeat, carry yourself with honor.
Win without boasting, lose without bitterness.
One day's outcome does not define a life – Ma'at weighs the total of your heart, not a single battle.
Help your fallen rival to his feet; there is more nobility in mercy than in triumph.
Do not delight in your enemy's downfall, lest the gods see and judge you by the same measure.
True honor is not in never falling, but in rising without malice each time you fall.
Your character in dark times is the test of your light.

THE CROWD
LI.

Do not simply follow the crowd; the path of the many is not always right.

Think for yourself and stand by justice, even if you stand alone.

Many hands can lift a load, but many voices can lead astray.

The jackal pack may howl at the moon, but their noise does not change its course.

Popularity is not the same as goodness.

Let principle guide you above popularity.

If others mock the truth, hold the truth tighter still.

Often the path of Ma'at is a narrow trail in the wilderness – firm beneath the feet, though few find it.

ACTION
LII.

Words are seeds; deeds are the fruit.
A promise means little until it is fulfilled.
Do not announce what you will do – do it, and let the work speak.
The wind carries off idle boasts, but the results of effort remain.
If you say you will help your brother, help him without delay.
If you commit to a task, see it through.
Many speak, few act; be among the few.
In the end, actions – not words – uphold Ma'at in this world.

BAD COMPANY
LIII.

Choose carefully whom you keep near your fire.
A quick-tempered friend will soon entangle you in needless flames.
A thief will make you complicit in his thefts.
One who laughs at injustice will dull your sense of right.
You cannot wholly avoid the wicked, but you need not make them your companions.
Better to walk alone than with a crowd running toward a cliff.
Your character is reflected in the company you keep.
Keep fellowship with the good, and even if trouble comes, you will not fall to disgrace.
Ma'at is preserved when you surround yourself with those who honor it.

TRUST
LIV.

Trust is a precious gift – give it wisely.
Not everyone who smiles at you is your friend.
It is good to trust in goodness, but also keep your eyes open.
A serpent may hide under the sweetest flower.
Yet a life without trust is a lonely field with no shelter.
So trust, but test; forgive, but remember.
Entrust your heart to those proven true.
Even then, know that humans are fallible and may fail you.
Place your ultimate trust in Ma'at, the eternal law of truth and balance, for it never falters.

DIGNITY
LV.

When provoked by insults or foolish talk, keep your dignity.
Flies cannot disturb calm water unless you let them.
If a lesser man shouts, answer him with silence or measured words.
To join his fury makes you his equal in folly.
Know your worth, and do not lower yourself to wrestle in mud.
There is strength in restraint: like an elephant beset by dogs, simply move on unmoved.
All will see who is noble and who is the fool.
In time, your composure will earn respect, while his fire burns to ash.

OPENNESS
LVI.

Be not rigid in your thinking – a tree that cannot bend will break in the storm.

Welcome new ideas and even criticism, as the river welcomes tributaries and grows.

Do not cling stubbornly to a course proven unwise; changing course can be wisdom, not weakness.

The ostrich hides its head and sees nothing – do not be like it.

Adapt to new truths as they reveal themselves. Stubborn pride in error serves no one.

Hold your convictions firmly, but not so tightly that they choke out truth.

Adjust your steps to stay in tune with Ma'at.

The wise remain ever a student of the world.

GRIEF
LVII.

Grief comes to all who love – it is the price of having a full heart.

Do not be ashamed of your tears for those you have lost; your tears honor them.

But do not let sorrow become your master.

The dead do not desire endless mourning; they have gone west, awaiting your smile again.

Speak of your loved ones with joy for the time you shared.

By remembering their deeds and speaking their names, you give them life among the living.

Your heart will heal in time, as the lotus closes at night and opens with the sun.

Ma'at teaches that all cycles – death to life, sorrow to hope.

Trust that the sun will rise even after the darkest night of grief.

FLATTERY
LVIII.

Beware the flatterer whose tongue drips honey but hides a knife.

Not all who praise you seek your good; some feed you sweet words to serve their own ends.

Value the friend who tells you a hard truth over the sycophant who tells you only what you wish to hear.

A mirror that lies about your reflection is worse than no mirror at all.

Do not let vanity deafen you to honest counsel.

Likewise, be sparing with flattery yourself – give praise only when earned.

Sincere words build trust; false praise builds traps.

Walk in truth and require truth from those around you – that is armor against deception.

PERSPECTIVE LIX.

When problems weigh you down, step back and look to the stars.
You will see your troubles shrink as your vision expands.
The stars have seen countless generations come and go; under their light, king and peasant are the same.
Remember how small you are in the vastness of creation – not to belittle your worth, but to right-size your worry.
The river still flows and the sun still rises, regardless of our daily triumphs or sorrows.
Find comfort in this steady rhythm.
Align yourself with the grand scheme of things, and your heart will find peace in its rightful place.

EVERYDAY MA'AT
LX.

Ma'at lives not only in royal decrees or temple rites,
but in the small daily choices of ordinary people.
Each time you choose kindness over cruelty, honesty over comfort,
you uphold Ma'at.
When you hold the door for a stranger, return a lost coin,
or refuse to join in gossip, the feather of Ma'at is present.
The strength of the world rests on countless small stones
of justice and compassion.
Even unseen, your good acts set one block upon another.
No righteous act is ever wasted, however humble.
Live each day by Ma'at in little ways,
and you become a living pillar of truth and balance.

RESPONSIBILITY LXI.

When things go wrong, the fool blames others, but the wise first examines themselves.
Take responsibility for your actions and their consequences.
If you have erred, admit it quickly and strive to mend the harm.
Blame is easy and solves nothing.
By owning your part in a problem, you gain the power to fix it.
Life hands you circumstances, but how you meet them is your choice.
Do not shirk duty or shift guilt.
Stand upright in both success and failure.
The load on your shoulders lightens when carried with honesty.
Ma'at supports those who stand accountable under its gaze.

COMPASSION
LXII.

Treat the vulnerable with care and respect.
Mock not the blind or the lame; dishonor not the old or the poor.
How one treats the powerless is the measure of a heart.
Remember, fortune's wheel turns – tomorrow you might be the one in need.
Extend a hand, not a sneer. The strong are meant to protect, not prey.
All people carry the spark of life and deserve dignity.
When you show compassion to those who suffer, you serve Ma'at itself.
A gentle touch and a kind word can heal unseen wounds.
By lifting another up, you rise as well in the eyes of eternity.

LAUGHTER
LXIII.

Laughter is medicine for the heart.
Do not be solemn beyond measure – the gods themselves enjoy a jest.
A moment of honest mirth can dispel a mountain of sorrow.
Learn to laugh at yourself kindly; it is a sign of wisdom.
A cheerful heart draws people as a fire draws the cold.
So long as your laughter harms no one and lightens the spirit, it is blessed.
In laughter we find our common humanity.
Even in hard times, a bit of humor is a lamp in the dark.
Ma'at smiles upon those who balance earnestness with joy.

GRATITUDE LXIV.

Let gratitude be your daily ritual.
At sunrise, give thanks for the light; at night, give thanks for rest.
The grateful heart turns even modest possessions into abundant blessings.
Do not focus on what is missing – cherish what is present.
Complaints furrow the face and invite bitterness to take root.
One who counts their blessings finds joy multiplied.
Thankfulness is wine for the soul: drink it and see the world shine.
Even in hardship, find one thing to be thankful for; that spark will light your way out of darkness.
A grateful heart stays in balance with Ma'at.

SOLITUDE LXV.

Set counsel in the shrine within.
In quiet, the heart speaks.
Do not fear the lone hour.
The desert at dusk teaches the willing.
When a storm of words rises,
make a mooring post of your tongue.
Sleep on your speech.
Wind-swift talk passes. Truth remains.
Stand as the heron in still water.
Let clarity gather like stars.
Weigh your deeds and desires on the scale.
In the hush, Ma'at steps from the clamor.
Rise renewed, the heart set straight.

ONENESS
LXVI.

All things share one breath.
Earth, sky, water, creatures, and we –
currents within the same great river.
Tug one current and the banks feel it;
no joy or sorrow stands alone.
See yourself in the stranger, the rival, the beast in the field.
Harm another and the wound returns;
help another and the blessing flows back.
A drop is not apart from the river.
Knowing this, walk gently; do no needless harm.
Ma'at is the unity that holds the many as one.
Live by Ma'at, and you honor all that is.

SELF-KNOWLEDGE LXVII.

The lotus needs water;
papyrus needs marsh.
Know your place of growth.
Be yourself,
not your neighbor's shadow.

EXCELLENCE LXVIII.

Whatever you do, do it with care and excellence.
A shoddy offering dishonors the maker more than the gods.
Your work reflects your spirit.
If you are a scribe, let your lines be true; if a builder, let each stone be firm.
Quality matters more than show.
Labor patiently, and let no detail be too small for your attention.
Through devoted craft, you partake in creation's perfection.
Even humble tasks gain dignity when done well.
By striving for excellence in your deeds, you bring Ma'at into the works of your hands and leave a legacy your soul can be proud of.

RENEWAL
LXIX.

No matter how far you have gone down a wrong road, you can always turn back.
Each morning the sun returns and with it a chance to begin anew.
Do not cling to past mistakes out of pride or despair.
Shed your old skin like a serpent and step again onto the path of Ma'at.
The gods are patient with those who sincerely change.
Apologize where needed, forgive yourself, and move forward.
As long as breath remains, hope remains for a better course.
A tarnished heart can be polished by honest effort.
Renewal is always possible – this mercy is woven into creation.

ACCEPTANCE LXX.

There are things in life you can change and things you cannot.
Wisdom is knowing one from the other.
After you have planted and tended, accept the field's yield.
After you have done your part in justice, accept that some outcomes lie with Ma'at and the gods.
Rail not against the inevitable – storms will come despite prayer; loved ones will depart despite tears.
Meet what you cannot alter with grace.
Acceptance is not surrender of goodness, but surrender of futile struggle.
By accepting what you cannot control, you find peace amid change.
In acceptance, your heart remains unbroken by the weight of the world.

REFLECTION LXXI.

The world is a mirror; the deeds you send out will return to you.

Show kindness and you invite kindness; deal cruelly and expect the same.

Do not do to another what you would not want done to you.

Your actions toward the weak and the stranger are the truest test of your character.

If you seek love, give love. If you desire respect, show respect.

The evil one does may seem to prosper at first, but in time misfortune finds its way home.

Likewise, every generosity you scatter will bloom in unexpected places.

All that you do circles back in time – walk accordingly under Ma'at's eye.

VIRTUE LXXII.

Do good for its own sake, not for praise or gain.
A righteous act loses grace if done for show.
The hidden good you do, the kindness no one sees – these are the purest offerings to Ma'at.
The wind does not applaud the tree for giving shade, yet the traveler is still comforted.
Do right even when no reward is in sight; that is when virtue truly lives.
Fame is fickle and gold loses its luster, but quiet goodness endures in the heart.
The soul nourished by virtue needs no audience.
Be your own witness to your integrity, and let that be enough.

ORDER LXXIII.

Ma'at thrives where order and respect prevail.
Respect just laws, for they frame peace.
Order is the vessel of truth.
Play your part as a citizen upholding what is right.
Defy not authority for pride's sake, yet neither obey unjust commands.
Offer honest counsel to those above if you can, but accept rightful decisions with grace.
When each person keeps their duty in harmony, the whole kingdom prospers.
Order is the vessel that carries truth – do not abandon it lightly.

EXAMPLE LXXIV.

Do not demand of others what you refuse to do yourself.
Rule yourself before you rule anyone else.
An unruly house cannot lead a village, just as an undisciplined person cannot guide others.
Lead by example, not by force.
If you want your children or students to be virtuous, show them virtue in your own life.
Correct your own faults before pointing out your neighbor's.
People are persuaded more by a life of honor than by a hundred loud proclamations.
Be to others a living model of Ma'at.
In your actions, let others see truth and balance, and they will be inspired to follow.

APPEARANCES LXXV.

Judge not a person by fine clothes or high position.
A heart of gold may beat under a tattered cloak, and a corrupt spirit may lurk behind a courtier's smile.
Outer beauty is fleeting; inner goodness is lasting.
The true measure of a human is in their deeds and words, not in their ornaments.
Do not be dazzled by titles or fooled by wealth.
A clay cup holds pure water as well as a golden chalice.
Honor virtue wherever it is found, even in the lowliest place.
See others with Ma'at's eyes, which peer straight into the heart.
You will find truth often wears humble garb.

INDUSTRY
LXXVI.

An idle hour is a treasure squandered.
Fill your time with purpose, learning, or kindness – not with idle gossip and lounging.
There is a time for rest, but let it be earned and brief.
The lazy postpone every duty and find life slipping away empty.
Work while it is day, so that when night comes you can sleep content.
Do not say "I will do it tomorrow," for too many tomorrows build only regret.
The bee gathers nectar while it can; the Nile's flood waits for no procrastinator.
Use your time and energy wisely to avoid remorse.
Diligence in youth brings comfort in old age; idleness brings only empty years.
Ma'at favors the active, engaged heart.

COUNSEL LXXVII.

Seek advice from the wise who have walked the road before you.
Pride can deafen us to good guidance.
Even a king needs counsel; even a sage listens to another voice.
Consider the counsel of the experienced, then decide your course.
Do not be ashamed to ask directions when lost – the road to truth is found by seeking.
Surround yourself with honest advisers, not merely those who agree with you.
Listen also to the counsel of your own conscience in quiet moments.
With many counselors, plans are strengthened; with none, they falter.
Heed good counsel and you add the knowledge of others to your own.

UNDERSTANDING LXXVIII.

Approach difference with curiosity, not judgment.
The world is wide, and Ma'at embraces many faces.
Scorn not what you do not understand.
One man eats dates, another eats figs – both are nourished.
Hold to the truth as you see it, yet allow others their path if it brings no harm.
Debate with civility; disagree without hatred.
Often, beneath differing words and customs, the same heart beats.
Find common ground where you can; where you cannot, offer respect.
Know that not everyone is your mirror – wisdom grows from that knowing.
Unity is not uniformity; Ma'at builds harmony as many stones form one pyramid.

THE SCALES
LXXIX.

Imagine the scales in the Hall of Truth: on one side, your heart; on the other, the feather of Ma'at.
A heavy heart, laden with wrongdoing, tips the balance against you.
A light heart, free of malice and regret, rises and passes the test.
Each day, weigh your own heart in quiet reflection.
Remove what weighs it down – anger, deceit, greed – one by one.
Feed it virtues that make it feather-light – kindness, honesty, peace.
Do this, and when the final judgment comes you will have no fear.
Your heart will be light as the feather of Ma'at, and you will pass into the Field of Reeds justified.

MA'AT LXXX.

Ma'at is the eternal law, the heartbeat of the cosmos.
It is not merely written in papyrus or carved in stone; it is woven into the fabric of creation.
Ma'at is the rightness that makes the stars travel their courses and the Nile flood in season.
It is as soft as a feather and as firm as a mountain's base.
You cannot hold Ma'at in your hand, yet it upholds all.
It has existed since the first dawn and will endure beyond the last dusk.
To live in Ma'at is to live in tune with the music of the divine.
In truth, Ma'at is the Way itself – the path of balance, justice, and harmony that sustains the world.

THE SAGE LXXXI.

The sage of Ma'at lives quietly and without strife.
They nurture justice in their heart and need no boast on their lips.
They step aside from credit, letting good deeds be their own reward.
Untroubled by anger and untouched by greed, the sage moves through life like water: gentle and unstoppable.
They give without keeping account, lead without dominating, teach without condescension.
When success comes, they smile and move on; when failure comes, they learn and move on.
In company, they are gracious; in solitude, they are content.
The sage carries Ma'at in their breast as a living flame.
By their presence, the world is made lighter, yet they claim no glory.
They are like a tree giving shade – all benefit, and the tree does not proclaim its virtue.
Empty of ego and full of compassion, the sage lives in harmony with all.
In them, the Way of Ma'at finds its purest expression.

www.ingramcontent.com/pod-product-compliance
Lightning Source LLC
Chambersburg PA
CBHW051700040426
42446CB00009B/1225